MUSHROOMS IN THE POCKET

EMPTYING THE EMOTIONS FROM MY POCKET OF EXISTENCE

AISHWARYA VEDULA

I dedicate this book to my parents, my better half for their constant patience and love for me.

And to my beloved teachers, wonderful peers who still encourage me to capture instances and to curate a memoir of memories.

Contents

Preface *vii*

Dusted Dreams

Bemused Brainstorming

An Afternoon Art

Lost Letters

Remorsing Reverence

Immaculate Indifferences

Hidden Hell

Something? Some? Thing?

Committing Chat

Heavenly Hell

Nurture Nothing

Supersede The Shine

Matter Of Me

I In The Eye

Slit Of The Sight

Soul In The Shower

Pestered By Palette

War Of Words

Tick-Tock

Puzzled Ponder

Rant In Robotics

Preface

"The only difference between a garden and a graveyard is what you choose to put in"

-Rudy Francisco

Oh to be a poetry
bloom everyday
die everyday
Oh to be a poet
die one day
be remembered everyday

Dusted Dreams

A sense of yearning,
to pull a chair-
at the side of your bed
to watch you sleep.

Wrapping your ethereal body-
consisting of unshaved follicles,
with a satin blanket-
that is capable of seizing the sunshine.

Fabricating it as a viaduct,
for the delusion of this path-
woven by moonlight
between your curated dreams and my verity.

Myself being called as a crowded cursed city
with no infrastructure.
You, an isle with sacred water.

I desire to drown into,
the unstable tunnel-
of your liquify thoughts

To eradicate the mundane
perception of my relatively
distraught past.

Bemused Brainstorming

URGENT:
You have a class today—
the duopolies of the decade.
Let us answer your questions;
new ideas are ready for you.
What's next?

Here's a pocket-friendly SURPRISE:
you appeared in 3 searches this week—
sand, flesh, and sky.
3 persons visited your profile:
book, quote, art.

Here's a little letter from us to the
Lost Generation: A Satan You Can Love and Hate
(to Media, Journalists, local Political leaders).

What should we do
to secure the collective power of leadership?
A tale of intergalactic action.

Life is now easy—
Horizontally, 8 becomes infinity.

A self-test kit for just Rs. 250,
gift your mood: au naturel
amidst the rise of uncertainty.

Source: A remix / cut-up poem made from Email Subjects received in a day.

An Afternoon Art

On a summer afternoon
So softly, a tender breeze brush against my knees
After all the misses and confessions
I had all and then most of you

So softly, a tender breeze brushes against my knees
Some and now none of you
I had all and then most of you
I've heard it said, that beauty is when scars become art

Some and now none of you
Teach me to heal my scars
I've heard it said, that beauty is when scars become art
To the stars, that we never really owned as ours

Teach me to heal my scars
After all the misses and confessions
To the stars, that we never really owned as ours
On a summer afternoon

Source: A Pantoum composed from selected lines & phrases of song lyrics of *Honey Bee* by The Head and The Heart, *The Night We Met* by Lord Huron, *When Scars Become Art* by Gatton,

Sunkissed by Khai Dreams.

Lost Letters

I wrote

because

you never

listened.

Nevermind,

it

however ended up

bearing the burden

of

piled up

unsent letters.

Remorsing Reverence

Did I ever leave you?
But you certainly let me go.

You desired to print a palace—
to be locked away forever,
somewhere on the front page of trapped book.

Perhaps, you wished to protect me (or to hide me?) -
so they couldn't find me out of curiosity,
which they invariably preserve for the last page.

Immaculate Indifferences

While

searching

for

the

similarities

between

us,

I

fell

in

love

with

the

differences.

Differences that make us real,

differences that widen our scope.

Hidden Hell

Hell is never bound

to afterlife and chaos.

Everyday is hell

when life doesn't go

the way we want.

Something? Some? thing?

Something

left

between

us?

But

that something

isn't of us

anymore.

Committing Chat

Do you want to commit suicide?
Would you like to hear?
Is something happening?
You mean to say you don't know?
(Did I have to know all this before he could ask such a little thing?)
Would you like to hear?'
What do you think we stopped for—
to admire the view?!
What's your opinion of me, anyhow?
What do I owe you?
A little champagne?
What day would suit you?
Do you always watch for the longest day of the year and then miss it?
Oh, is that your suit?
Why don't we just go home?
Is it all quiet up there?
(What was the use of doing great things if I could have a better time telling what I was going to do?)

Source: Fitzgerald, F. Scott. The Great Gatsby. Wordsworth

Editions, 2019

Method: Questions Only Poem.

Heavenly Hell

Embroidery of clouds,

woven together by heaven.

Dancing thoughts in my mind,

imitating the flame.

When the provoked wind blows,

it carries hope.

Pattern of pictures

of people..

Voices of virtues

running down in our veins...

Nurture Nothing

Turn to an afterthought,

which would hold my stars.

Envy borrowed time—

we rip so much out of ourselves to be *n o t h i n g.*

Who said smiles are the metaphorical upholstery of serenity?

Little do we know, it is the cradle of *C h A o S.*

Supersede The Shine

Who dared to dim thy shine, sun?
Moon's monthly grave isn't that strong, they say.
I reckon,
my desired apogee superseded the conspiracy of the cosmos.

Oh thee beauty

Matter of Me

Matter or mould,
my existence,
a whole, or a hole?
Unaware and unseen,
of the milieu.

I in the Eye

Eyes transplantation—
the last serendipity
to see the world again

Slit of the Sight

Drowning in sclera,
the chaste.
Restraining in retina,
from falsifying perspectives.

Soul in the Shower

The last time I showered,
I fancied the art of falling in love… again.
I could not differentiate between my tears and the drops.
Perhaps, the only space where I can
let my emotions drain
with the fragranced soap water.
I wish my towel could be capable of soaking,
all the scars that you gave me.
The ones my body got imprinted with.
I just lay here, like the towel on a railing.,
All these emotions cherishing and sailing.
Our differences still haunt me,
like a cliff with no railings.

Pestered by Palette

Trapped in a tapestry,
with no gloss.
Forget the cosmos-
a single stroke can erase,
my entire esse.
Would they still care about the beaut?
After all these years of mastering-
the art of making a tear drop,
suppressing my tears in reality.
Muting the world to get,
my senses rewilded.

War of Words

Words are capable of changing histories.
The stories we hear,
time is the greatest eraser
of sorrows and of joy…

Who knows?
Beyond this oscillating world of pleasure and sorrow,
much has been written.
Perhaps that is the miracle of stories.
They make us resolute again,
stories of never imagined possibilities.

The battle between equals
--reality and imagination--
flatter them by calling them faultless,
like death and rebirth keep going.

Tick-Tock

Fetch the vault of knowledge,
beyond expected readiness.

Pause yourself,
because time answers our paralyzed worries

Puzzled Ponder

No one leaves home unless
the yellowed diary's notes whisper in vernacular.
"Is this how it's supposed to end?"

There in the attic of forgotten shapes,
I tend the mobile now like an injured bird.
It was hard to believe the flesh was heavy on my back.

I love all films that start with rain.
How on earth did it happen, I used to wonder…

Source: First-line, multi-author Cento poem, inclusive of several prominent authors' work

Rant in Robotics

White wire coo.
Stupid configuration sways.
Short circuit sighs.
The hollow plug teases.
A warm battery lulls me.
That sunken energy now floats.
A hideous malware swabs my stubborn safe gently.
And in all these levitating chaos.
I see a fully charged self.

9 798887 175300

Printed by Libri Plureos GmbH in Hamburg,
Germany